STORYLAND

3

Student's Book

Lisiane Ott Schulz
Luciana Santos Pinheiro

Storyland Student's Site Access Code:
Storyland3@students

Pearson

Head of Product - Pearson Brasil	Juliano Costa
Product Manager - Pearson Brasil	Marjorie Robles
Product Coordinator - ELT	Mônica Bicalho
Authors	Lisiane Ott Schulz
	Luciana Santos Pinheiro
Collaborators	Fernanda Bressan Capelini
	Indiana Oliveira
	Milena Schneid Eich
	Sofia Xanthopoulos Bordin
	Verônica Bombassaro
Editor - ELT	Simara H. Dal'Alba
Editorial Assistant - ELT	Sandra Vergani Dall'Agnol
Proofreader	Silva Serviços de Educação
Proofreader (Portuguese):	Fernanda R. Braga Simon
Copyeditor	Maria Estela Alcântara
Teacher's Guide (Portuguese translation)	Eduardo Lubisco Portella
Pedagogical Reviewer	Viviane Kirmeliene
Quality Control	Renata S. C. Victor
Product Design Coordinator	Rafael Lino
Art Editor - ELT	Emily Andrade
Production Editors	Daniel Reis
	Vitor Martins
Acquisitions and permissions Manager	Maiti Salla
Acquisitions and permissions	Sandra Sebastião
Graphic design	Mirella Della Maggiore Armentano
	APIS design integrado
Graphic design (cover)	Daniel Reis
	Emily Andrade
	Mirella Della Maggiore Armentano
Illustration (cover)	Leandro Marcondes
Illustrated by	Alex Cói | Estúdio Secreto
	Bruna Sousa
	Bruno Badain | Manga Mecânica
	Leandro Marcondes
	Marcelo Kina
	Mari Heffner
Content Development	Allya Language Solutions
Media Development	Estação Gráfica
Audio	Maximal Studio

Every effort has been made to trace the copyright holders and we apologize in advance for any unintentional omissions. We would be pleased to insert the appropriate acknowledgement in any subsequent edition of this publication.

Dados Internacionais de Catalogação na Publicação (CIP)
(Câmara Brasileira do Livro, SP, Brasil)

Schulz, Lisiane Ott
 Storyland 3: Student's Book / Lisiane Ott Schulz, Luciana Santos Pinheiro ; [coordenação Monica Bicalho]. -- 1. ed. -- São Paulo : Pearson Education do Brasil, 2018.

Vários ilustradores.
ISBN 978-85-430-2637-4

1. Inglês (Educação infantil) I. Pinheiro, Luciana Santos. II. Bicalho, Monica. III. Título.

18-17182   CDD-372.21

Índices para catálogo sistemático:
1. Inglês : Educação infantil 372.21
Maria Alice Ferreira - Bibliotecária - CRB-8/7964

ISBN 978-85-430-2637-4 (Student's Book)

STORYLAND

Student's Book 3

UNIT 1	The Lion And The Mouse	8
UNIT 2	Snow White	16
UNIT 3	Aladdin	24
UNIT 4	The Giant Turnip	32
UNIT 5	The Bremen Town Musicians	40
UNIT 6	Little Red Riding Hood	48
UNIT 7	Yankee Doodle	56
UNIT 8	The Princess And The Pea	64

Press-outs 73

Stickers 89

Scope and Sequence

UNIT	THEME	VALUES	OBJECTIVES	MAIN LANGUAGE	SONG	CLIL
1 The Lion And The Mouse	We are all special	Help other people; Value people's efforts. Be friends with others	• Distinguish between *big* and *little*, *up* and *down*, and *sleep* and *wake up*	big, down, little, sleep, up, wake up; play, see-saw, slide, swing	The more we get together	Drama: Act out the story
2 Snow White	Hygiene and Housekeeping	keeping things neat and clean, helping others	• Distinguish between *clean* and *dirty*, *neat* and *messy*, and *open* and *close* • Count to seven	make the bed, set the table, wash your hands; clean, close, dirty, messy, neat, open; one, two, three, four, five, six, seven	Here we go round the mulberry bush	Science: Learn how not to spread germs
3 Aladdin	Transportation	Respect traffic rules	• Identify and name means of transportation • Learn about traffic rules	airplane, boat, bus, car, train; driver; green, red, yellow; go, slow down; stop;	The wheels on the bus	Art & Social Studies: Make a means of transportation
4 The Giant Turnip	Family	Work together to reach a goal	• Name family members • Follow commands • Count to eight	dad, daughter, husband, mom, son, wife; one, two, three, four, five, six, seven, eight; big, small; hop, run, stop, walk	Walking, walking	P.E.: Play tug of war

UNIT	THEME	VALUES	OBJECTIVES	MAIN LANGUAGE	SONG	CLIL
5 The Bremen Town Musicians	Animals and Music	Show respect for the elderly; Take good care of animals	• Identify and name animals • Identify and name musical instruments	cat, cow, dog, donkey, rooster, sheep; cry; band, drums, guitar, musicians, violin	Little Boy Blue	Music: Make a rubber band guitar
6 Little Red Riding Hood	Parts of the Body and the Senses	Respect family rules and someone's privacy	• Identify and name parts of the face • Relate parts of the body to their senses	ears, eyes, mouth, nose; eat, hear, listen, see, smell, taste	Two little eyes to look around	Social Science: Understand the senses with a sensory shoe box
7 Yankee Doodle	Clothes	Keep yourself tidy	• Identify and name pieces of clothing • Name colors • Count to ten	boots, hat, pants, jeans, scarf, shirt, shoes, shoelaces, T-shirt; colors; five, six, seven, eight, nine, ten; He is wearing a brown hat	One, two, buckle my shoe	Fine Motor Skills: Tie your shoelace
8 The Princess And The Pea	Good and Bad Manners	Behave at the table	• Identify cutlery items and learn how to use them • Identify members of a royal family • Count to ten	cup, fork, knife, napkin, spoon; hard, soft; king, queen, prince, princess; six, seven, eight, nine, ten	Baa, baa, black sheep	Drama: Make a tea party

We are in Storyland

7

UNIT 1 — The Lion And The Mouse

LESSON 1

1 LOOK AND CIRCLE.

2 LISTEN AND STICK. TRACK 03

LESSON 1

STORY

3 LISTEN AND REPEAT. THEN MATCH.

TRACK 04

LESSON 2

4 FIND AND COLOR.

LESSON 2

11

5 LOOK, LISTEN, AND SING.

TRACK 05

LESSON 3

SING

6 GLUE.

LESSON 3

1	2	3
4	5	6

7 LISTEN AND CIRCLE. THEN COLOR.

TRACK 06

LESSON 4

8 CUT AND COLOR. THEN ACT OUT.

DRAMA CLIL

LESSON 4

UNIT 2 SNOW WHITE

1 LOOK AND CIRCLE.

Lesson 1

2 LISTEN AND STICK.

TRACK 07

LESSON 1

STORY

3 LISTEN. THEN CIRCLE.

TRACK 08

LESSON 2

4 MATCH. THEN SAY.

Lesson 2

MESSY

DIRTY

OPEN

NEAT

CLEAN

CLOSE

5 LISTEN AND SING.

TRACK 09

LESSON 3

SING

6 LISTEN AND GLUE. TRACK 10

LESSON 3

1	2	3
4	5	6

7 DRAW.

LESSON 4

8 LEARN HOW NOT TO SPREAD GERMS.

SCIENCE CLIL — LESSON 4

23

UNIT 3 ALADDIN

Lesson 1

1 LOOK AND CIRCLE.

2 LISTEN AND STICK.

TRACK 11

LESSON 1

STORY

25

3 TRACE AND SAY.

CAR

BOAT

AIRPLANE

TRAIN

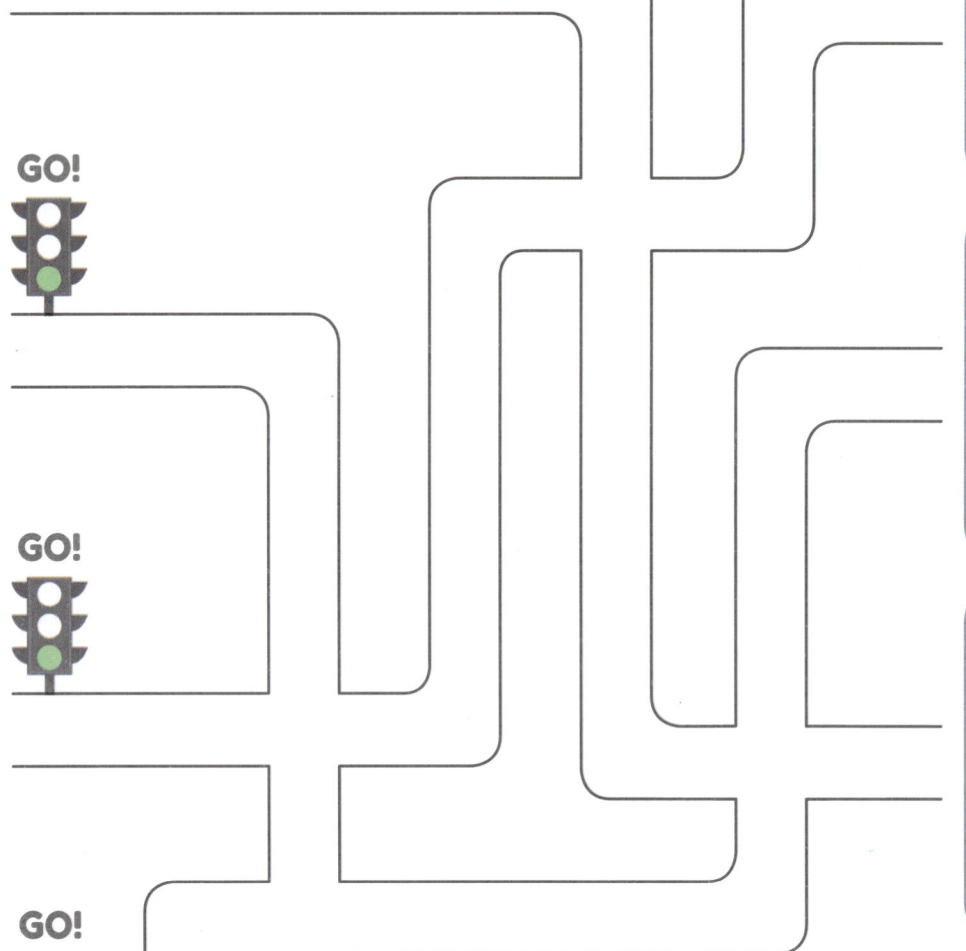

4 LOOK AND SAY. THEN COLOR.

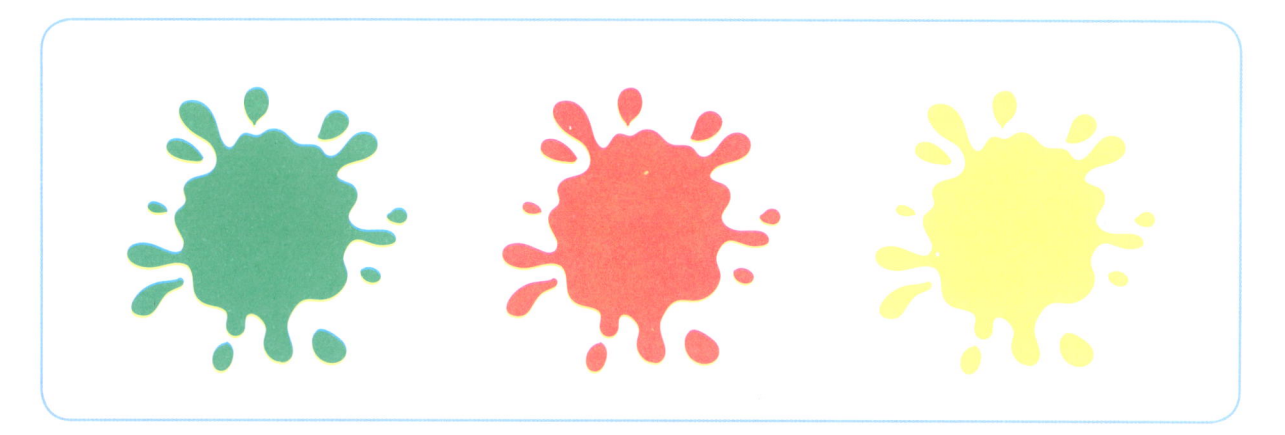

LESSON 2

STOP

SLOW

GO

5 LOOK, LISTEN, AND SING.

TRACK 12

LESSON 3

SING

SCHOOL BUS

6 CUT, LISTEN, AND GLUE.

TRACK 13

LESSON 3

1	2	3
4	5	6

7 SING AND ACT OUT.

TRACK 14

SING

LESSON 4

8 MAKE A MEANS OF TRANSPORTATION.

ART & SOCIAL STUDIES CLIL

LESSON 4

UNIT 4 The Giant Turnip

LESSON 1

1 LOOK, SAY, AND CIRCLE.

2 LISTEN AND STICK.

TRACK 15

LESSON 1

3 CUT, LISTEN, AND ACT OUT.

TRACK 16

LESSON 2

4 LISTEN AND POINT. TRACK 17

BIG

SMALL

Lesson 2

5 LISTEN AND SING. THEN COLOR.

TRACK 18

LESSON 3

6 CUT, MATCH, AND PLAY.

LESSON 3

7 COUNT AND CIRCLE.

	3 4 5
	5 6 7
	6 7 8
	7 8 6

8 PLAY TUG OF WAR.

P.E. CLIL LESSON 4

UNIT 5 — THE BREMEN TOWN MUSICIANS

LESSON 1

1 LOOK AND CIRCLE.

2 LISTEN AND STICK.

TRACK 19

STORY

LESSON 1

41

3 CUT AND GLUE.

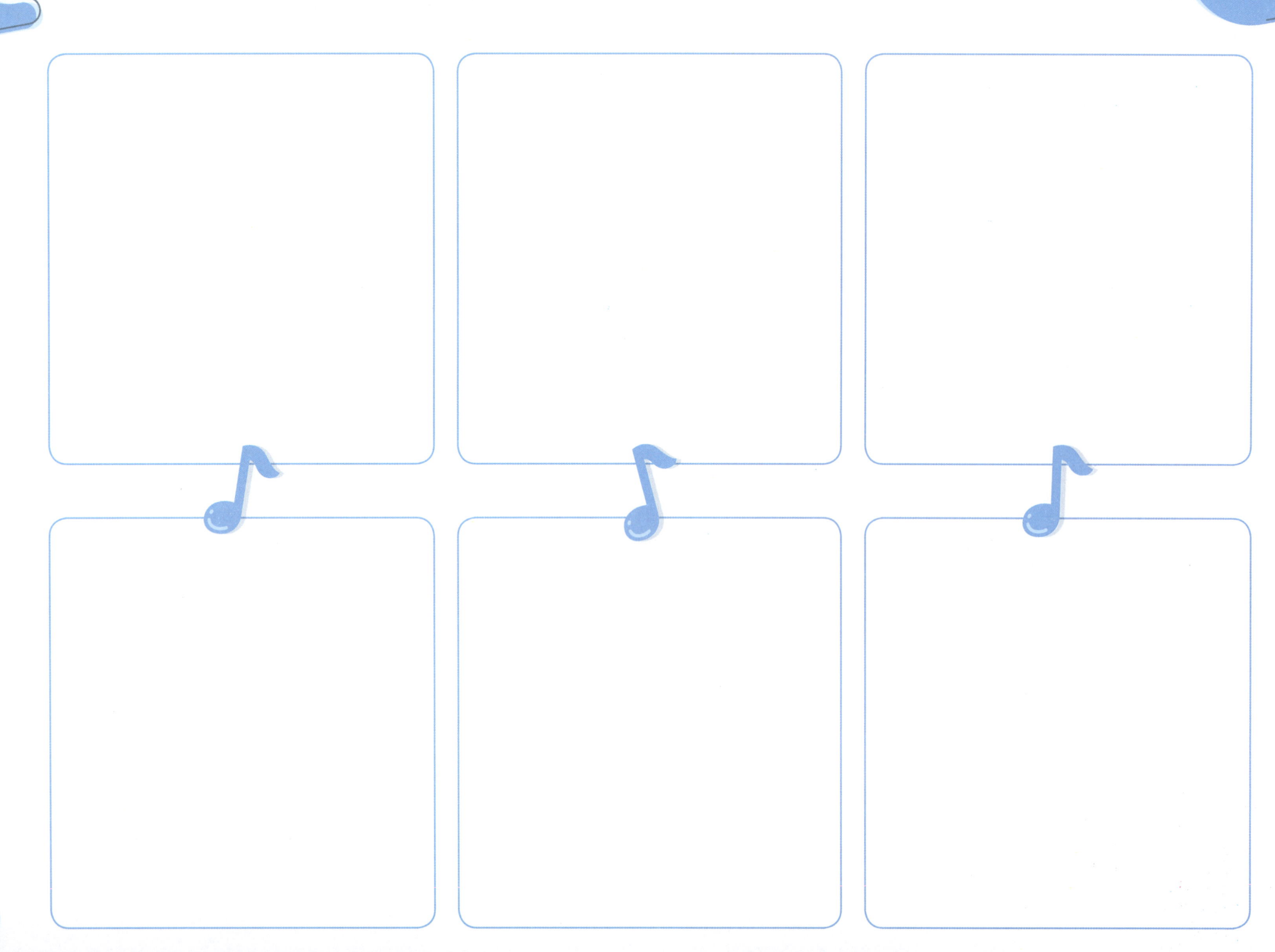

Lesson 2

4 LISTEN AND COLOR.

TRACK 20

LESSON 2

5 LISTEN AND MATCH. TRACK 21

Lesson 3

1

2

3

6 LISTEN, SING, AND ACT OUT.

TRACK 22

LESSON 3

SING

7 LOOK AND TRACE.

LESSON 4

8 MAKE A RUBBER BAND GUITAR.

MUSIC CLIL — LESSON 4

47

UNIT 6 LITTLE RED RIDING HOOD

LESSON 1

1 LOOK AND STICK. THEN LISTEN.

TRACK 23

STORY

2 LISTEN AND CIRCLE.

TRACK 24

LESSON 1

49

3 LOOK AND DRAW.

LESSON 2

4 LOOK AND MATCH.

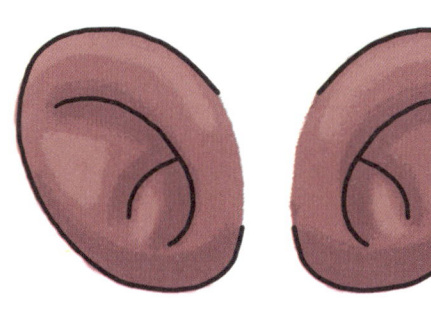

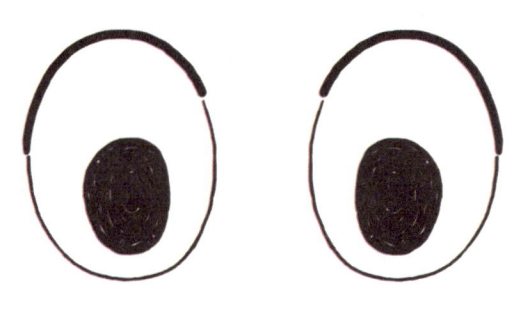

Lesson 2

5 LISTEN AND ACT OUT.

TRACK 25

LESSON 3

6 LISTEN AND SING.

TRACK 26

LESSON 3

SING

7 CUT, LISTEN, AND GLUE.

TRACK 27

LESSON 4

1	2	3
4	5	6

8 LEARN ABOUT THE SENSES WITH A SENSORY SHOE BOX.

SOCIAL SCIENCE CLIL

LESSON 4

UNIT 7 YANKEE DOODLE

LESSON 1

1 LOOK AND STICK.

2 LISTEN AND COLOR. TRACK 28

LESSON 1

STORY

3 MATCH AND COLOR.

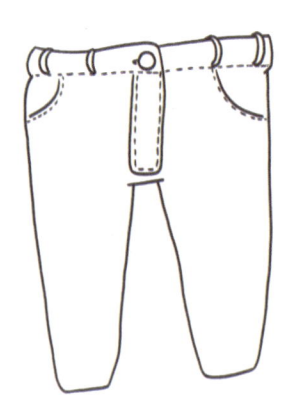

LESSON 2

4 MATCH AND SAY.

LESSON 2

5 LISTEN AND SING. THEN COLOR.

TRACK 29

LESSON 3

6 CUT, PLAY, AND GLUE.

LESSON 3

5	6	7
8	9	10

7 LISTEN, SING, AND ACT OUT.

TRACK 30

SING

LESSON 4

8 TIE YOUR SHOELACE.

FINE MOTOR SKILLS CLIL

Lesson 4

63

UNIT 8 The Princess And The Pea

LESSON 1

1 LISTEN AND STICK.

TRACK 31

2 LOOK, COUNT, AND COLOR.

LESSON 1

STORY

3 CUT AND GLUE.

LESSON 2

1	2	3
4	5	6

4 TRACE, COLOR, AND COUNT.

LESSON 2

5 LISTEN AND COLOR. THEN SING. TRACK 32

LESSON 3

SING

6 LISTEN AND CIRCLE.

TRACK 33

LESSON 3

7 COUNT AND SAY.

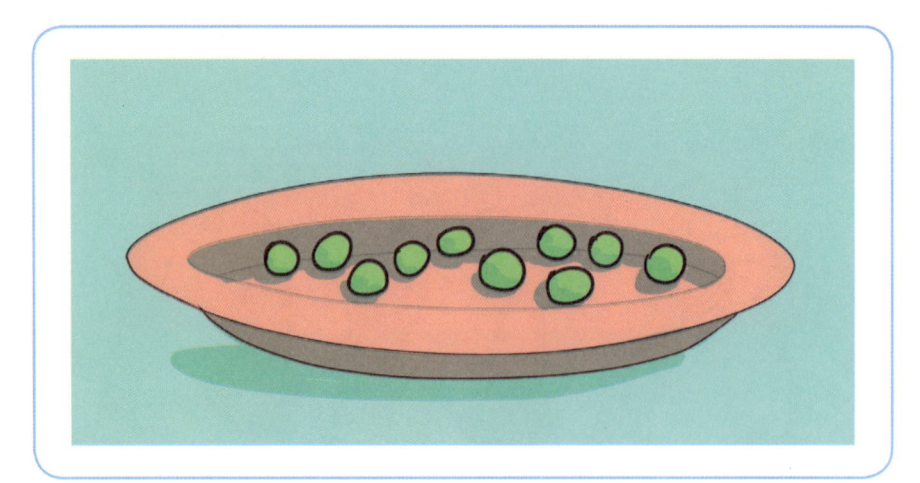

8 MAKE A TEA PARTY.

TEA PARTY

Press-outs & Stickers

Press-outs

UNIT 1

Press-outs

Unit 2

Press-outs

UNIT 3

Press-outs

UNIT 4

Press-outs

UNIT 6

Press-outs

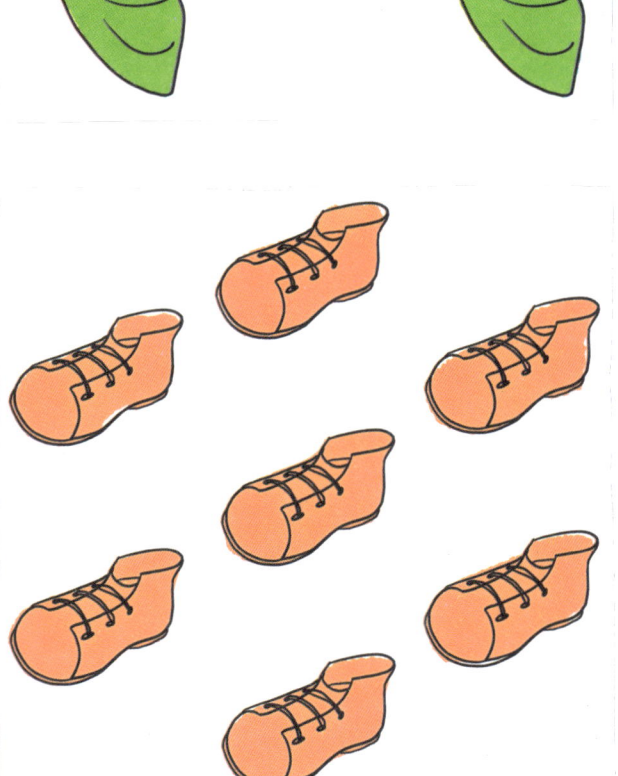

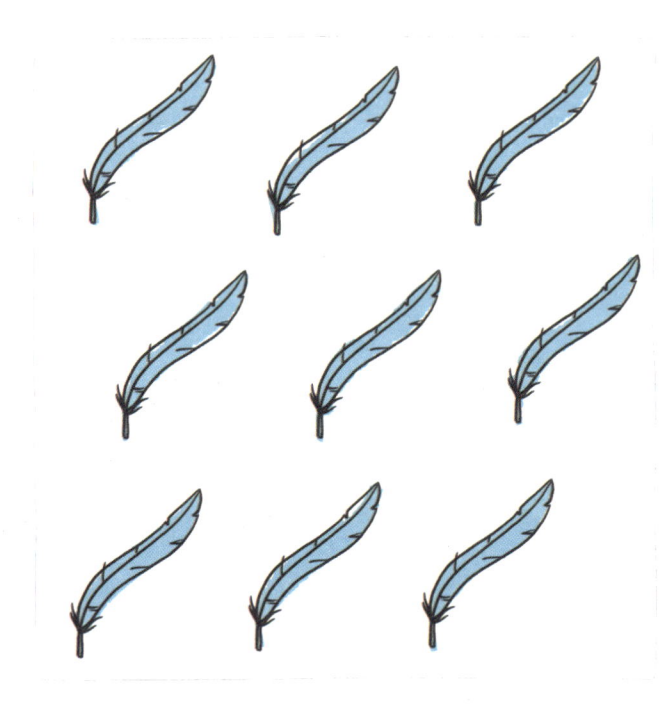

UNIT 7

Press-outs

UNIT 8

Stickers

UNIT **1**

UNIT **2**

Stickers

UNIT 3

UNIT 4

Stickers

Unit 5

Unit 6

Stickers

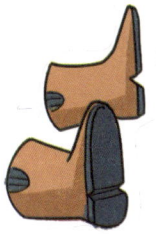

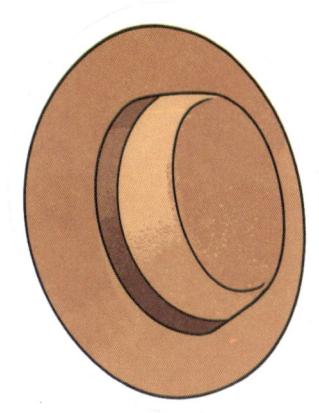

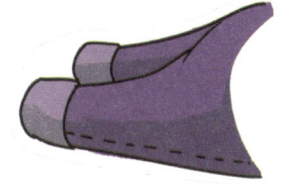

UNIT 7

UNIT 8

Cover Stickers

97